Date: 5/19/11

J 302.22 BEL
Bell-Rehwoldt, Sheri.
Speaking secret codes /

EDGE BOOKS

MAKING AND BREAKING CODES

# SPEAKING SECRET CODES

BY SHERI BELL-REHWOLDT

Consultant:
Professor Mihir Bellare
Department of Computer Science and Engineering
University of California, San Diego

CAPSTONE PRESS
a capstone imprint

Edge Books are published by Capstone Press,
151 Good Counsel Drive, P.O. Box 669, Mankato, Minnesota 56002.
www.capstonepub.com

Printed in the United States of America in North Mankato, Minnesota.
032010
005740CGF10

 Books published by Capstone Press are manufactured with paper
containing at least 10 percent post-consumer waste.

*Library of Congress Cataloging-in-Publication Data*
Bell-Rehwoldt, Sheri.
  Speaking secret codes / by Sheri Bell-Rehwoldt.
      p. cm.—(Making and breaking codes)
  Includes bibliographical references and index.
  Summary: "Discusses different methods for speaking secret
codes"—Provided by publisher.
  ISBN 978-1-4296-4569-0 (library binding)
  1. Languages, secret—Juvenile literature. I. Title. II. Series.

PM9001.B45 2011
302.2'2—dc22                                          2010004163

## EDITORIAL CREDITS

Mandy Robbins, editor; Ted Williams, designer; Marcie Spence,
    media researcher; Laura Manthe, production specialist

## PHOTO CREDITS

Alamy/WorldFoto, 9; AP Images, 14; Newscom/AFP Photos/HO, 13;
Newscom/AFP Photo/Saul Loeb, 26; Reuters/Corbis, 24; Shaun Curry/
AFP/Getty Images Inc., 25; Shutterstock/26kot, 27; Shutterstock/
AVAVA, 21; Shutterstock/Coia Hubert, 7; Shutterstock/Elena Elisseeva,
8; Shutterstock/Katrina Brown, cover; Shutterstock/Lisa F. Young, 16;
Shutterstock/Monkey Business Images, 4, 6; Shutterstock/Rudyanto
Wijaya, 28; Shutterstock/Steve Lovegrove, 19; Shutterstock/tandem, 18;
Shutterstock/Yuri Arcurs, 22; Time Life Pictures/Library of Congress/
Getty Images Inc., 11; Workbook Stock/Getty Images Inc., 20

# TABLE OF CONTENTS

# ALL LANGUAGE IS CODE

Did you know there are about 5,000 spoken languages in the world? All spoken languages are codes. Take the English language, for example. To people who don't understand it, it's gibberish.

Most languages are created to enable people to understand each other. But sometimes people create codes to hide secret messages. When people send and receive these messages, they become code talkers. Code talkers need two things: the code and the key. The code locks the message. The key or **cipher** unlocks it.

Spoken codes have been used throughout history during times of war. They have also been used by thieves and prisoners of war. Today, doctors, truckers, and even police officers use spoken codes. Anyone can create a spoken code, including you!

**cipher**—a secret system that changes messages into secret code

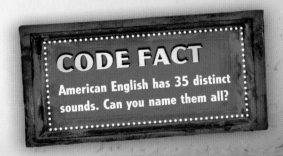

## CODE FACT
American English has 35 distinct sounds. Can you name them all?

# CHAPTER 1

# LEARNING ABOUT LANGUAGE

Speaking in code can be tricky. If you don't have the key in front of you, you may make some mistakes at first. But remember that learning usually follows failure, especially when it comes to language.

Think of babies learning to speak. Long before they can use whole sentences, they do a lot of listening. Babies also do a lot of practicing, which often sounds like meaningless babble. And when babies first start speaking, they make a lot of mistakes.

## A MUSICAL CODE

Sheet music is a type of code that starts out silent. But when the music is decoded by someone playing an instrument, it becomes a song. To someone who doesn't know how to read it, sheet music looks like a bunch of dots and lines. To someone who knows how to read music, it is the key to creating a song.

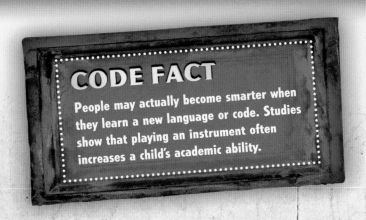

### CODE FACT

People may actually become smarter when they learn a new language or code. Studies show that playing an instrument often increases a child's academic ability.

# WHAT'S SPECIAL ABOUT SPOKEN LANGUAGE?

The way a language is spoken gives clues about those speaking it. The English spoken in Great Britain sounds very different from American English. Even within the United States, people speak differently. We can tell where people are from just by their accents or particular words they use. People in Minnesota, for example, take drinks out of a water fountain. But in parts of Wisconsin, this machine is called a bubbler. People in Southern states will ask if you want a coke when they offer you a soft drink. In other parts of the country, the same beverage would be called a pop or a soda.

Some languages sound very melodic. They have a lot of changes in pitch or tone. A word's meaning could change depending on these tones. Many American Indian languages work this way. In the Navajo language, nearly every word contains syllables with high and low tones. Say the same word one way, and it means one thing. But say it another way, and it means something totally different. Because Navajo is so difficult to learn, it has been used as an effective code.

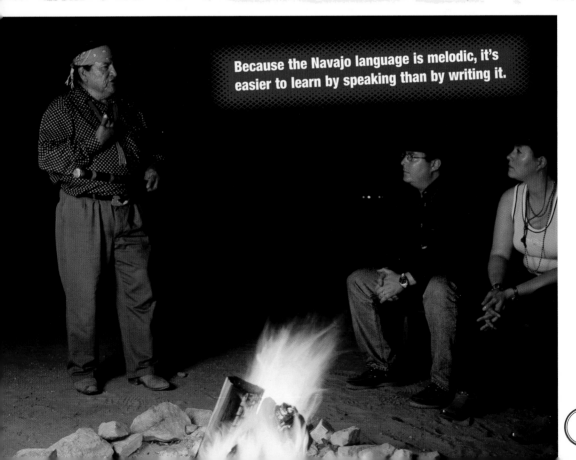

Because the Navajo language is melodic, it's easier to learn by speaking than by writing it.

# CHAPTER 2

# SPOKEN CODES IN HISTORY

Codes have actually changed the course of history. Wars have been won or lost with the help of codes. Rulers have taken power or been overthrown. Some codes have even saved lives. This was true for African slaves traveling the Underground Railroad during the Civil War (1861–1865).

## UNDERGROUND RAILROAD

The Underground Railroad was a network of secret routes and houses used by slaves to escape to freedom. Slaves were not allowed to learn to read or write. So they created code words based on the railroad. The word "baggage" meant slaves, and "stations" meant safe houses. People willing to risk their lives to help the slaves were called "conductors."

Slaves also sang songs to tell each other they were going to escape. Slaves sang, "I'm bound for heaven," if they planned to escape to Canada. The code words allowed the slaves to communicate within earshot of their owners.

Harriet Tubman was a well-known Underground Railroad conductor.

## TRY YOUR OWN SONG CODE

You may not be fleeing to freedom, but you can create your own song code. Maybe you and your friend are playing a trick on someone. Your friend is waiting to drop a water balloon on your brother's head. You stand on the sidewalk outside, while your friend hides near an upstairs window. Just when your brother is below the upstairs window, you can start singing a song. That's the cue for your friend to drop the water balloon.

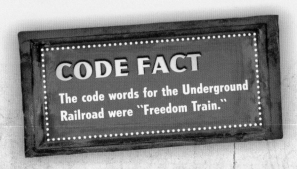

### CODE FACT
The code words for the Underground Railroad were "Freedom Train."

# NAVAJO CODE TALKERS

During World War II (1939–1945), the United States military fought the Japanese. U.S. military leaders had trouble creating a code that the Japanese couldn't crack.

Eventually, the United States recruited American Indians from the Navajo tribe to create a secret military code. The Navajo language has only four vowels, but each has many **intonations**. The code allowed the Navajo code talkers to communicate military words like "machine gun" and "submarine."

For greater secrecy, the code wasn't written down. Code talkers memorized it. Throughout the war, the Japanese never cracked the code. With the help of the Navajo code talkers, the United States captured the island of Iwo Jima. The capture of this important Pacific island helped the U.S. win the war.

**intonation**—a change in the way a sound is made that can affect a word's meaning

Navajo code talkers sent their messages over radios.

## WORD SUBSTITUTION

The Navajo language doesn't include any military words. Code talkers had to create code words for common military items. They based their code words on nature. The code word for "submarine" was "iron fish." That is *besh-lo* in the Navajo language.

You may not speak another language, but you too can use terms from nature in your own spoken code. You could call a motorcycle "rolling thunder." A backpack could be called a turtle shell. Perhaps a secret message is a "whispering wind."

## TAP CODE

Sometimes people must find other ways to communicate when they can't use their voices. During the Vietnam War (1959–1975), U.S. prisoners of war (POWs) tapped coded messages. The tap code allowed them to outsmart their Vietnamese jailers. POWs tapped to discuss what to say if they were questioned by the guards. They also tapped to find out if other POWs were hurt. The tap code helped POWs keep up their spirits because they knew others cared about them.

POWs in Vietnam were rarely allowed to speak to each other.

To create the tap code, the English alphabet was put in a grid of five rows and five columns. The letter "K" was deleted to make the alphabet fit. The letter "C" replaced "K." After memorizing the chart, the prisoners would tap two numbers to represent a letter. The first number represented the rows. The second number represented the columns. Using this chart, the letter "J" would be 2-5. The letter "P" would be 3-5. The letter "X" was used to separate sentences.

|   | 1 | 2 | 3 | 4 | 5 |
|---|---|---|---|---|---|
| 1 | A | B | C | D | E |
| 2 | F | G | H | I | J |
| 3 | L | M | N | O | P |
| 4 | Q | R | S | T | U |
| 5 | V | W | X | Y | Z |

## CODE FACT

American POWs also used the tap code to have a bit of fun. At night they often tapped out DLTBBB. Can you guess what it means?

☑ *See page 32 for answer.*

# CHAPTER 3

# WORKING CODES

Some of the most famous codes in history were used during times of war. But today, many people still use codes in their jobs. When people substitute one word for another, or even a whole sentence, they create a **substitution** code. These codes are often used by professionals to keep the public from panicking.

## POLICE 10-CODES

Police departments use 10-codes to talk on their radios. When dispatchers notify police officers of a "10-32," they might mean "man with gun." But 10-codes are not **universal**. Each police department decides what their 10-codes mean. So "10-70" might mean "fire" to Chicago police officers. To officers in San Diego, it could mean "prowler." Often multiple agencies respond to an emergency. Differing 10-codes cause confusion. The U.S. Department of Homeland Security wants to do away with 10-codes. They want to create a universal code to eliminate confusion and miscommunication between emergency crews.

**CODE FACT**

Some police departments are switching to speaking plain English. They hope it will cut down on confusion during an emergency.

**substitution**—using a letter, number, or symbol to represent something other than its original meaning

**universal**—something that is shared by everyone

# HOSPITAL COLOR CODES

Hospitals use color codes so staff can react quickly to emergencies without upsetting hospital visitors. Hospital codes are usually based on colors. "Code Black" might mean "bomb threat." "Code Amber" could mean "missing child." "Code Silver" might mean "dangerous person with a weapon."

Color codes are great because they can be communicated visually and through speech. Blue could be your code word for "I've got a secret to tell

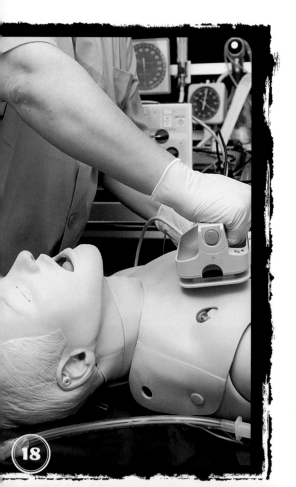

you." Imagine you are at a party with a friend. Saying "code blue" will let your friend know you have a secret to tell them away from the other guests. Your friend could even be all the way across the room. All you have to do is make eye contact and then point to a blue object. Your friend will soon come over to get the scoop.

## RETAIL CODES

Some businesses use codes for their own protection. Stores may use codes that help them catch thieves. Video cameras are placed around the store and are monitored by workers. A worker who spots a thief will broadcast a coded message over the store's speaker system. Then a security guard can catch the thief before he or she takes off with the merchandise.

## CODES ON THE ROADS

One well-known code is used by people on the move. Truck drivers share coded messages over their Citizens' Band (CB) radios. CB radios are based on **radio frequencies**. They can be used in areas with poor cell phone reception.

**radio frequency**—the frequency of the waves transmitted by a specific radio station

Truck drivers often have code names or "handles." Some examples are "Big Daddy" and "Rubber Ducky."

Can you guess the meaning of this sentence?

**"Back down, Rubber Ducky. Smokey's coming up behind us."**

☑ *See page 32 for answer.*

You can take a tip from truck driver code when you talk on the phone. Perhaps you're talking to a friend about a gift for your mom. "Smokey's coming up behind me" could mean, "I can't talk now. Mom is right behind me."

# CHAPTER 4

# FUN WITH CODES

There's no limit to the fun you can have speaking in codes. Some spoken codes have been enjoyed by generations of kids. You can speak some of these standard codes or have fun coming up with your own.

# PIG LATIN

When people mix up letters in a word, they create a **transposition** cipher. Pig Latin is a popular kids' code that uses transposition. It's simple but effective when spoken quickly.

**transposition**—rearranging the order of items in something

**1.** If a word starts with one or more consonants, move the consonants to the end of the word. Then add the sound "ay." "My dog" becomes "ymay ogday."

**2.** If a word with one syllable starts with a vowel, add "yay" to the end of the word. In doing this, "it" becomes "ityay," and "ear" becomes "earyay."

**3.** If a word has multiple syllables and starts with a vowel, add 'ay' to the end of it. "Apple" becomes "appleay" and "elephant" becomes "elephantay."

Can you decode this sentence?
**"Iyay amyay eakingspay igPay atinLay!"**

☑ *See page 32 for answer.*

# IDIOT CODES

When only the people using a code know what it means, it is called an "idiot code." Why? Because those who overhear it are clueless as to what's being said. Security experts think the terrorists who attacked the World Trade Center and the Pentagon on September 11, 2001 used them. The terrorists changed the meanings of common American words. For example, "bird" might actually have meant "airplane."

**The 9-11 terrorists**

Al Suqami  Waleed M. Alshehri  Wail M. Alshehri  Alomari  Atta

Moqed  Almihdhar  Nawaf Alhazmi  Salem Alhazmi  Hanjour

Alghamdi  Al Haznawi  Alnami  Jarrah

Al-Shehhi  Alghamdi  Al Qadi Banihammad  Hamza Alghamdi  Alshehri

It is easy to create your own idiot code. You can even go with a theme. If you're a Harry Potter fan, build a code from words in the novels. You could say, "He's a Potter," to mean someone is smart. Or maybe "Sure do love that Hogwart!" means "I really like your bike!"

## COCKNEY RHYMING SLANG

Cockney Rhyming Slang is a coded language used by people in the East End of London. Some people believe it started as a way for thieves to hide their plans from the police.

Cockney uses word combinations. The last word usually rhymes with the coded meaning. Many code phrases are more than 100 years old. But new phrases are frequently added. One phrase, "apples and pears," means "stairs." "Pie and mash" means "cash." Often, the rhyming word is left off. So a user might ask, "Got any pie?" if he needs a few dollars. A new phrase, "Barack Obama" means "charmer," as in "He's a right Barack."

Some Cockney phrases have been tested in a few London cash machines. Users of the kiosks had to know that "bladder of lard" meant ATM card and "Huckleberry Finn" meant Personal Identification Number, or PIN.

# CODES TO SUIT YOUR STYLE

Don't be afraid to personalize the codes you create. If you enjoy bird watching, why not create a code based on birds? "Yellow bird" could mean "Come over after school." "Dead bird" could mean "I'm grounded." Other people will think you and your friends are just discussing your hobby.

## WHITE HOUSE WHO'S WHO

The White House Communications Agency uses single-word code names for the first family. President Obama's code name is Renegade. Michelle Obama's is Renaissance. Malia's and Sasha's code names are Radiance and Rosebud.

All first family code names begin with the same letter. In the past, these codes were kept secret. Now they are used to provide clarity on who is being referenced. Without the code, someone referring to "Obama" would cause confusion. Agents would wonder which family member is being talked about.

If you're a music lover, you could even create a code from songs. When you're upset with your parents, hum a song instead of yelling and getting in trouble. Your parents won't have a clue, but you and your friends will. Or maybe sing a single note. Your code for "Get me out of this!" could be to hum, "Me-Me-Me!"

## TIPS FOR TOUGHER CODES

You can use more complicated techniques to make your code tougher to crack. Give your tongue a workout by speaking your code backward. Suppose your code for "sleep over" is "cats meow." When you say, "Thginot woem stac," your friends will know you're really saying, "Sleep over tonight."

You could also make your code trickier by speaking in acronyms. IMHO usually means "In my humble opinion." You could change it to mean "I'm gonna be sick!" And AFAIK, which normally means, "As far as I know" could mean "Food fight!" You can find lists of acronyms on the Internet. To get really clever, use the acronyms to make new words that start with the same letters.

As you can see, the sky is the limit when it comes to creating codes. You can write them, tap them, sing them, and speak them. Codes will be around for as long as people need to share secret messages.

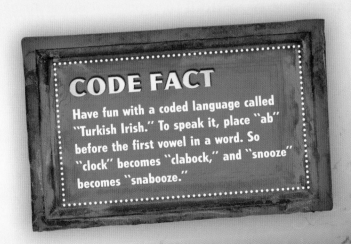

## CODE FACT

Have fun with a coded language called "Turkish Irish." To speak it, place "ab" before the first vowel in a word. So "clock" becomes "clabock," and "snooze" becomes "snabooze."

# GLOSSARY

**acronym** (AK-ruh-nim)—a word made from the first or first few letters of the words in a phrase

**cipher** (SY-fuhr)—a secret system that changes messages into secret code

**intonation** (in-tuh-NAY-shuhn)—a change in pitch or tone in a spoken language

**radio frequency** (RAY-dee-oh FREE-kwuhn-see)—the frequency of the waves transmitted by a specific radio station; radio waves are electromagnetic waves caused by electricity and magnetism

**substitution** (sub-stuh-TOO-shun)—using a letter, number, or symbol to represent something other than its original meaning

**transposition** (trans-puh-ZIH-shun)—rearranging the order of items in something

**universal** (yoo-nuh-VUR-suhl)—something that is shared by everyone

# READ MORE

**Gregory, Jillian.** *Making Secret Codes.* Making and Breaking Codes. Mankato, Minn.: Capstone Press, 2011.

**Lambert, David, and the Diagram Group.** *Super Little Giant Book of Secret Codes.* New York: Sterling Publishing Co., Inc., 2007.

**Lassieur, Allison.** *The Underground Railroad: An Interactive History Adventure.* Mankato, Minn.: Capstone Press, 2008.

# INTERNET SITES

FactHound offers a safe, fun way to find Internet sites related to this book. All of the sites on FactHound have been researched by our staff.

Here's all you do:

Visit *www.facthound.com*

Type in this code: 9781429645690

# INDEX

## ☑ ANSWERS

**PAGE 15:** *Don't let the bedbugs bite.*

**PAGE 21:** *Slow down, Rubber Ducky, a cop is following us.*

**PAGE 23:** *I am speaking Pig Latin!*